The best of
RICK
SPRINGFIELD

contents

PIANO • VOCAL • GUITAR

the greatest songs of the
Rock Era

ISBN-13: 978-1-4234-1705-7
ISBN-10: 1-4234-1705-4

HAL•LEONARD®
CORPORATION
7777 W. BLUEMOUND RD. P.O. BOX 13819 MILWAUKEE, WI 53213

Visit Hal Leonard Online at
www.halleonard.com

AGAINST ALL ODDS
(Take a Look at Me Now)

Words and Music by
PHIL COLLINS

Moderately slow

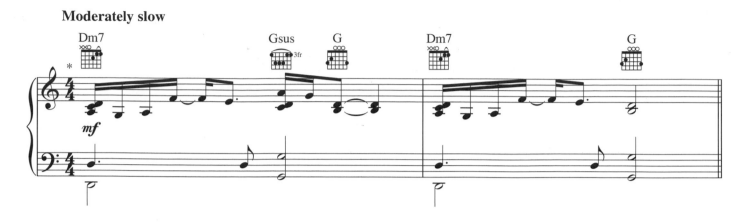

How can I just let you walk a-way, just let you leave with-out __ a trace, when I

stand here tak - ing ev - 'ry breath __ with you? _____ Ooh. _____ You're the

* Recorded a half step lower.

well, there's just an emp-ty space,_____ and you com-ing back___
'cause there's just an emp-ty space._____ But to wait_

___ to me_____ is a-gainst___ the odds,___ and that's what_____ I've got___ to face._____
___ for you_____ is all_____ I can do,___ and that's what_

I ___ I've got___ to face._____ Take a good look at me now,_

BEST OF MY LOVE

Words and Music by JOHN DAVID SOUTHER,
DON HENLEY and GLENN FREY

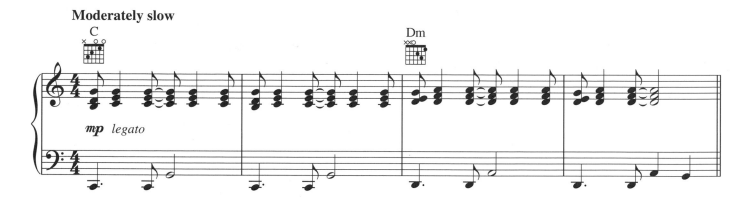

Ev-er-y night __ I'm ly-in' in bed, _____ hold-in' you close __ in my

Beau-ti-ful fac-es and loud emp-ty plac-es, look at the way that we

dreams; __ think-in' a-bout __ all the things that we __ said __ and

live; ___ wast-in' our time __ on cheap talk and wine

AMERICAN PIE

Words and Music by
DON McLEAN

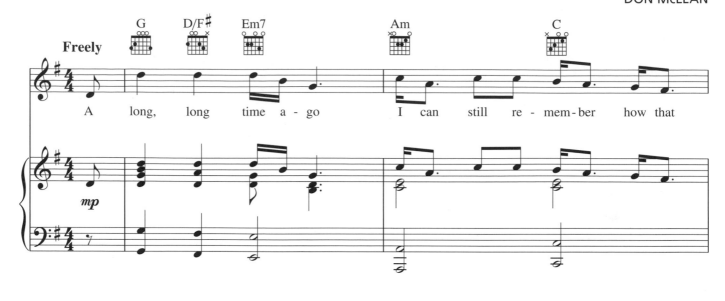

A long, long time a-go I can still re-mem-ber how that

mu-sic used to make me smile. _____ And

I knew if I had my chance that I could make those peo-ple dance and

Em   D7

This-'ll be the day __ that I ___ die. _____

Freely

G   D/F#   Em7   Am   C

I met a girl who sang __ the blues _____ and I asked her for some hap-py news, _____ but

Em   D

she just smiled ___ and turned a - way. _____

G   D/F#   Em   G/B   Am   G/B   C

I went down to the sa-cred store _____ where I heard the mu-sic years be-fore, but the

rit.

D.S. al Coda

day the mu - sic died. And they were sing - in'

CODA

this - 'll be the day ___ that I ___ die. ___

Additional Lyrics

2. Now for ten years we've been on our own,
   And moss grows fat on a rollin' stone
   But that's not how it used to be
   When the jester sang for the king and queen
   In a coat he borrowed from James Dean
   And a voice that came from you and me
   Oh and while the king was looking down,
   The jester stole his thorny crown
   The courtroom was adjourned,
   No verdict was returned
   And while Lenin read a book on Marx
   The quartet practiced in the park
   And we sang dirges in the dark
   The day the music died
   We were singin'...bye-bye... etc.

3. Helter-skelter in the summer swelter
   The birds flew off with a fallout shelter
   Eight miles high and fallin' fast,
   It landed foul on the grass
   The players tried for a forward pass,
   With the jester on the sidelines in a cast
   Now the half-time air was sweet perfume
   While the sergeants played a marching tune
   We all got up to dance
   But we never got the chance
   'Cause the players tried to take the field,
   The marching band refused to yield
   Do you recall what was revealed
   The day the music died
   We started singin'... bye-bye...etc.

4. And there we were all in one place,
   A generation lost in space
   With no time left to start again
   So come on, Jack be nimble, Jack be quick,
   Jack Flash sat on a candlestick
   'Cause fire is the devil's only friend
   And as I watched him on the stage
   My hands were clenched in fits of rage
   No angel born in hell
   Could break that Satan's spell
   And as the flames climbed high into the night
   To light the sacrificial rite
   I saw Satan laughing with delight
   The day the music died
   He was singin'...bye-bye...etc.

CALL ME
from the Paramount Motion Picture AMERICAN GIGOLO

Words by DEBORAH HARRY
Music by GIORGIO MORODER

Col - or me ___ your col - or, ba - by, col - or me ___ your car. ___ Col - or me ___ your col - or, dar - ling, I know who ___ you are. ___

CANDLE IN THE WIND

Music by ELTON JOHN
Words by BERNIE TAUPIN

DANCING QUEEN

Words and Music by BENNY ANDERSSON,
BJÖRN ULVAEUS and STIG ANDERSON

Strong Rock

You can dance. _ You can jive, _____ hav-ing _ the time of _ your life. ____ Oh, _____ see that _ girl. _

Watch that ___ scene, ___ dig-gin' the danc - ing ___ queen. ___

Dig-gin' the

danc - ing ___ queen. _____

Repeat and Fade

DREAMS

Words and Music by
STEVIE NICKS

EBONY AND IVORY

Words and Music by
PAUL McCARTNEY

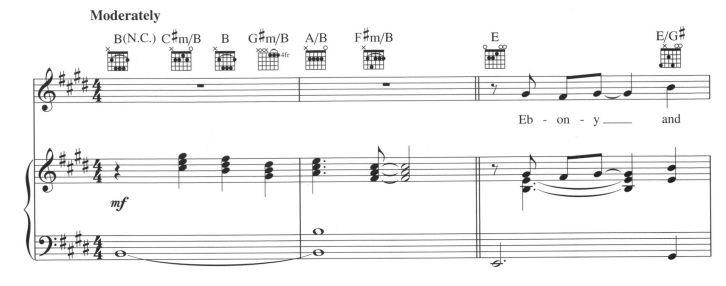

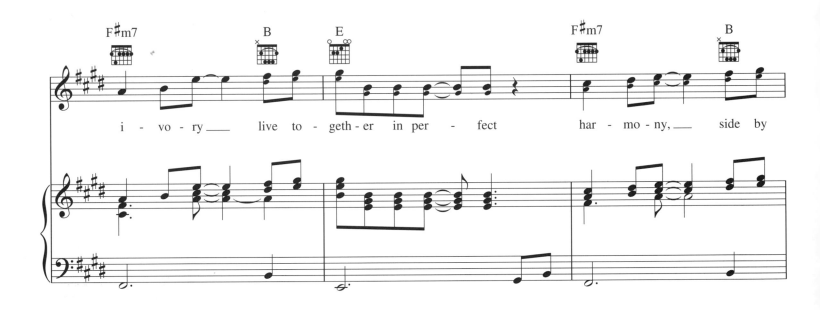

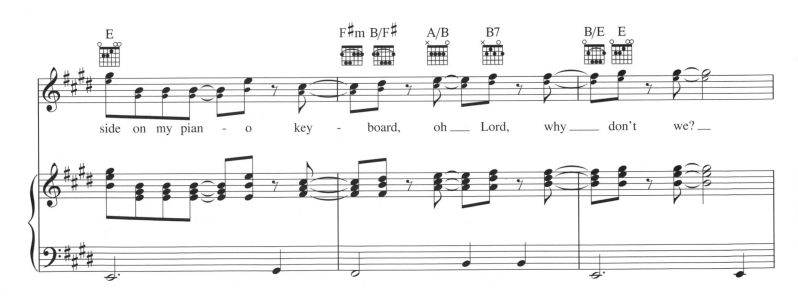

Eb - on - y, _____ i - vo - ry, _____

liv - ing in per - fect har - mo - ny. _____ Ooh.

(Everything I Do)
I DO IT FOR YOU

Words and Music by BRYAN ADAMS,
ROBERT JOHN LANGE and MICHAEL KAMEN

Look in - to my eyes, _____
Look in - to your heart, _____

you will see _____ what you mean to _____ me.
you will find _____ there's noth - ing there to _____ hide.

Search your
Take me as I

heart, _____ search your soul, _____ and when you
am, _____ take my life, _____ I would

ENDLESS LOVE

Words and Music by
LIONEL RICHIE

EVERY BREATH YOU TAKE

Music and Lyrics by
STING

67

69

EYE OF THE TIGER

Theme from ROCKY III

Words and Music by FRANK SULLIVAN
and JIM PETERIK

So man - y times __ it hap - pens too fast. _____
Face to face, __ out in the heat, _____
Ris - in' up, __ straight to the top. _____

You trade your pas - sion for glo - ry.
hang - in' tough, stay - in' hun - gry.
Had the guts, got the glo - ry.

Don't lose your grip __ on the
They stack the odds, __ still we
Went the dis - tance. Now I'm

dreams of the past. You must fight just to keep them a - live. __
take to the street for the kill with the skill to sur - vive. __
not gon - na stop, just a man and his will to sur - vive. __

FLASHDANCE...WHAT A FEELING

from the Paramount Picture FLASHDANCE

Lyrics by KEITH FORSEY and IRENE CARA
Music by GIORGIO MORODER

cried ____ si - lent tears ____ full of pride _____ in a

Faster, with a driving beat

world ____ made of steel, ____ made of stone. _____

— ____ Well, ____

I _____ hear the mu - sic, close my eyes, feel the
I _____ hear the mu - sic, close my eyes, I am

FOOTLOOSE

Theme from the Paramount Motion Picture FOOTLOOSE

Words by DEAN PITCHFORD and KENNY LOGGINS
Music by KENNY LOGGINS

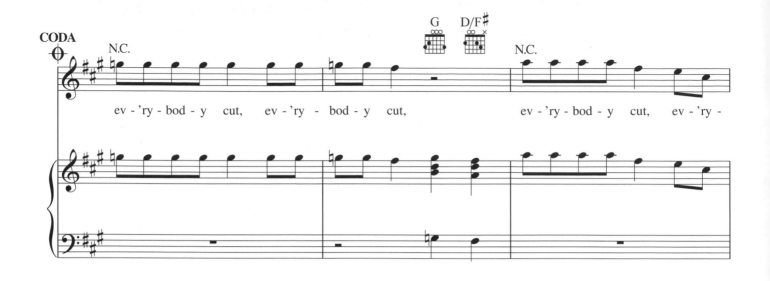

ev - 'ry - bod - y cut, ev - 'ry - bod - y cut, ev - 'ry - bod - y cut, ev - 'ry -

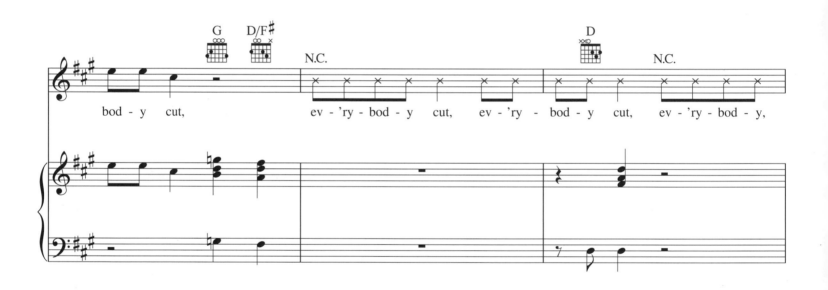

bod - y cut, ev - 'ry - bod - y cut, ev - 'ry - bod - y cut, ev - 'ry - bod - y,

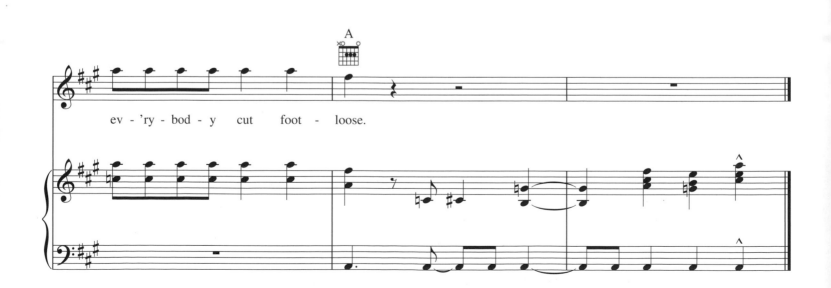

ev - 'ry - bod - y cut foot - loose.

HOW DEEP IS YOUR LOVE

from the Motion Picture SATURDAY NIGHT FEVER

Words and Music by BARRY GIBB,
ROBIN GIBB and MAURICE GIBB

GLORY OF LOVE
Theme from KARATE KID PART II

Words and Music by DAVID FOSTER,
PETER CETERA and DIANE NINI

I will al-ways love you, ___ I will nev-er leave you ___ a-lone. ___

Some-times I just for-get, say things I might re-gret, ___
You keep me stand-ing tall, you help me through it all, ___

it breaks my heart ___ to see ___ you cry - ing.
I'm al-ways strong ___ when you're ___ be - side me.

HEY JUDE

Words and Music by JOHN LENNON
and PAUL McCARTNEY

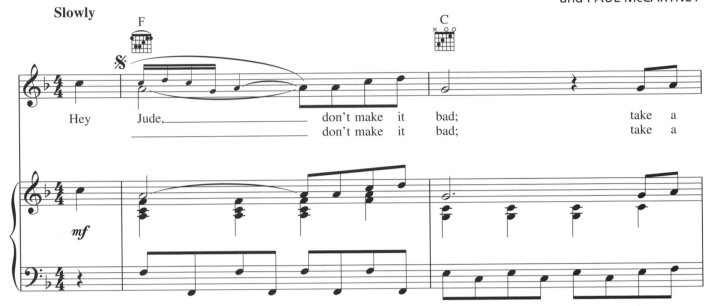

HOW AM I SUPPOSED TO LIVE WITHOUT YOU

Words and Music by MICHAEL BOLTON
and DOUG JAMES

I SHOT THE SHERIFF

Words and Music by
BOB MARLEY

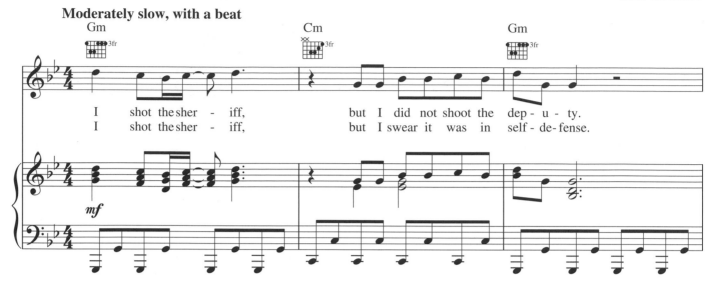

I shot the sher - iff, but I did not shoot the dep - u - ty.
I shot the sher - iff, but I swear it was in self - de - fense.

I shot the sher - iff, but I did - n't shoot the
I shot the sher - iff, and they say it is a

dep - u - ty.
cap - i - tal of - fense.

All a - round in my
Sher - iff John Brown al - ways

I GET AROUND

Words and Music by BRIAN WILSON
and MIKE LOVE

Medium bright Rock beat

I get a-round ___ from town to town. ___

___ I'm a real cool head, ___ I'm mak-in' real good bread. ___

I'm get-tin' bugged driv-in' up an' down the
al-ways take my car 'cause it's

I HEARD IT THROUGH THE GRAPEVINE

Words and Music by NORMAN J. WHITFIELD
and BARRETT STRONG

I SWEAR

Words and Music by FRANK MYERS
and GARY BAKER

I see the ques - tions in ___ your eyes; ___   I know what's weigh -

I'll give you ev - 'ry - thing ___ I can; ___   I'll build your dreams ___

For bet - ter or worse,___ till death do us part,_____ I'll

love you with ev - e - ry beat ___ of my heart, ___ I swear.___

_ of my heart,_ I swear._ *Instrumental solo*

I'D DO ANYTHING FOR LOVE
(But I Won't Do That)

Words and Music by
JIM STEINMAN

Moderately fast

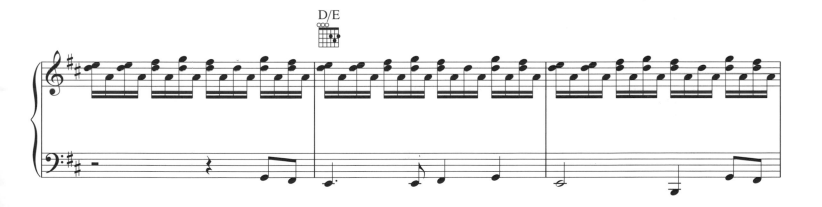

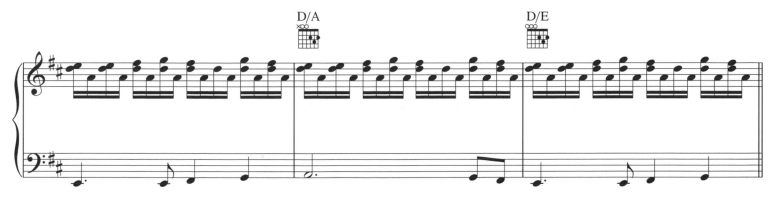

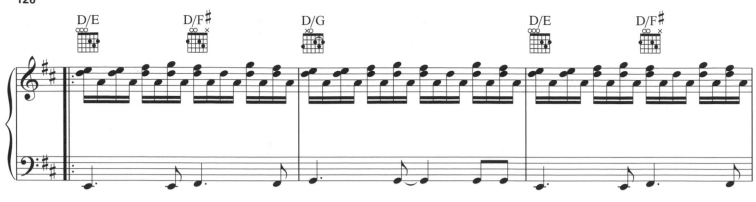

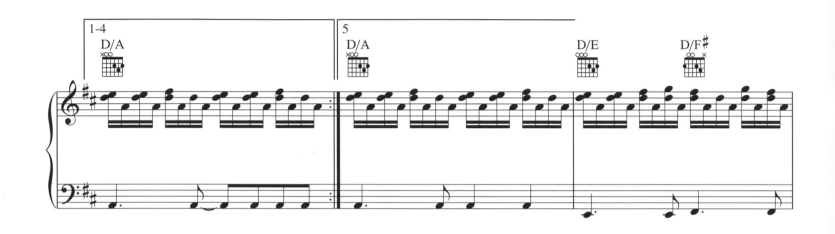

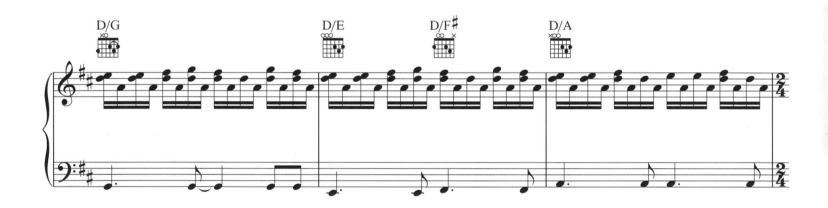

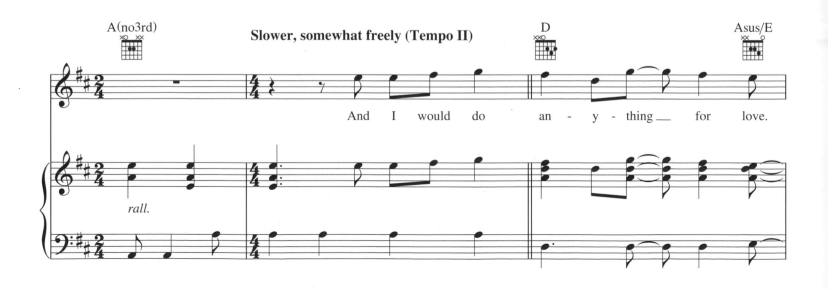

And I would do an-y-thing __ for love.

rall.

I WRITE THE SONGS

Words and Music by
BRUCE JOHNSTON

I'M A BELIEVER

Words and Music by
NEIL DIAMOND

love, and I'm a be - liev - er! I could - n't

leave her if I tried.

To Coda ⊕

D.S. al Coda

I'M YOUR ANGEL

Words and Music by
ROBERT KELLY

Slowly ♩ = 66

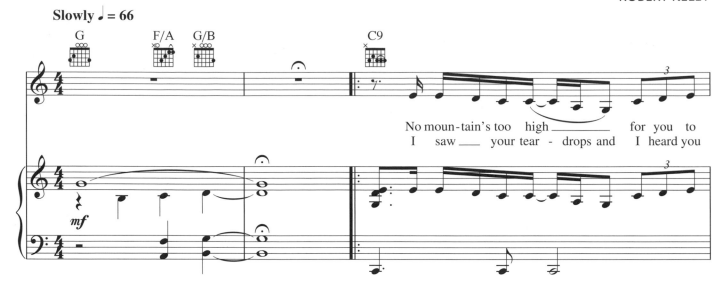

No moun-tain's too high _____ for you to
I saw _____ your tear - drops and I heard you

climb. _____ All _____ you have _____ to do _____ is have _____ some climb-
cry. _____ All _____ you need _____ is time. _____ Seek me and you _____

- ing faith, _____ oh, yeah. _____ No riv-er's too wide _____ for you to
_____ shall find. _____ You have ev - 'ry - thing _____ and you're still

JACK AND DIANE

Words and Music by
JOHN MELLENCAMP

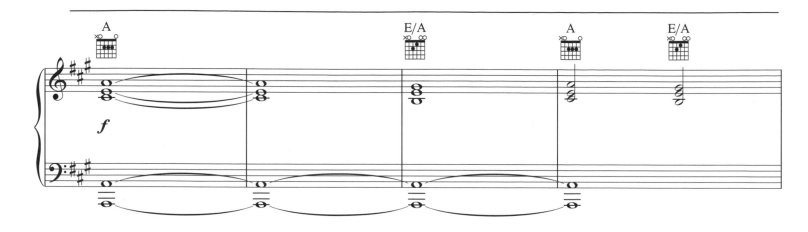

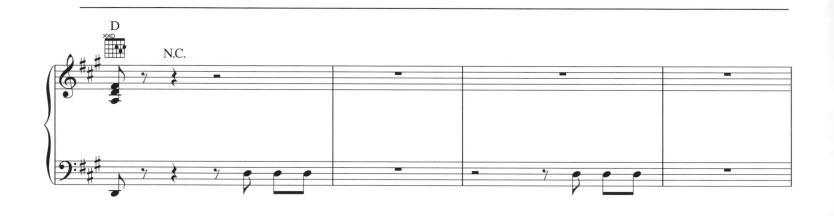

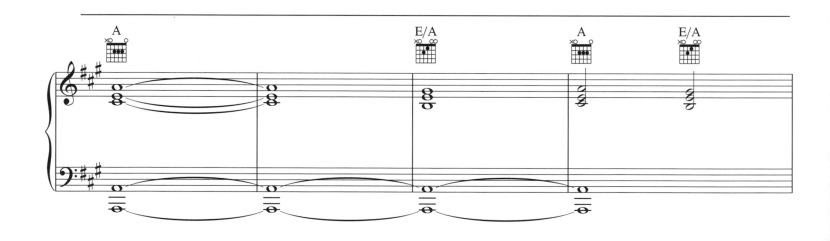

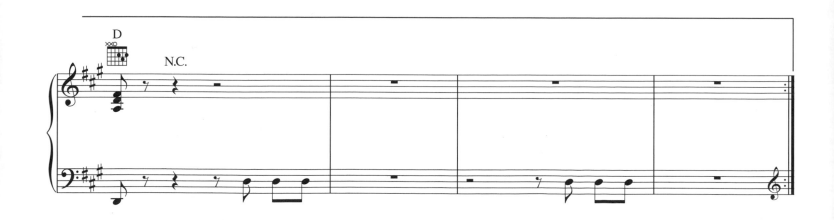

change is com - in' 'round real soon, make us wom - en and men.

D.S. al Coda

CODA

A lit - tle

Repeat and Fade

IT'S STILL ROCK AND ROLL TO ME

Words and Music by
BILLY JOEL

Moderately fast

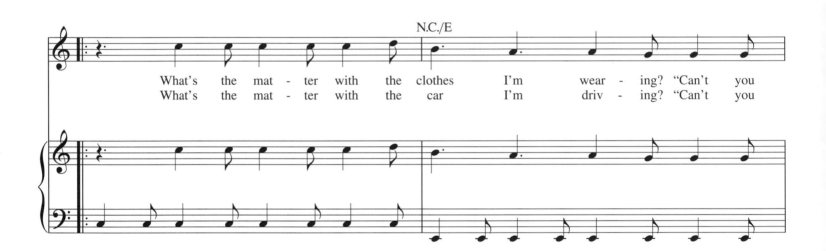

What's the mat - ter with the clothes I'm wear - ing? "Can't you
What's the mat - ter with the car I'm driv - ing? "Can't you

tell that your tie's too wide?" ___
tell that it's out of style?" ___

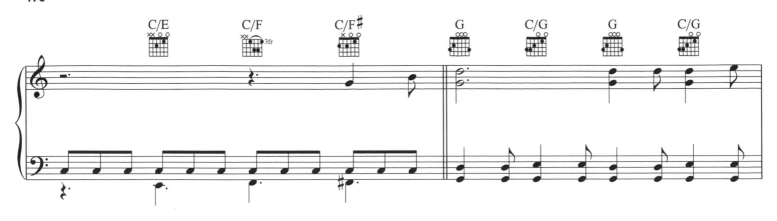

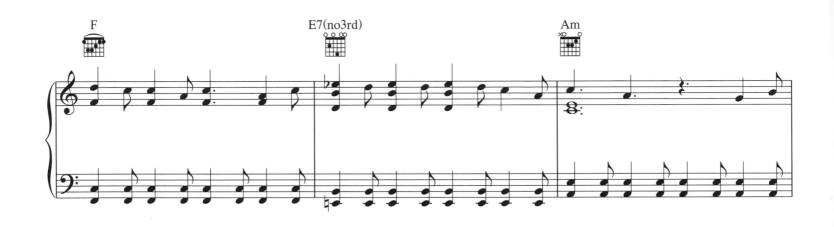

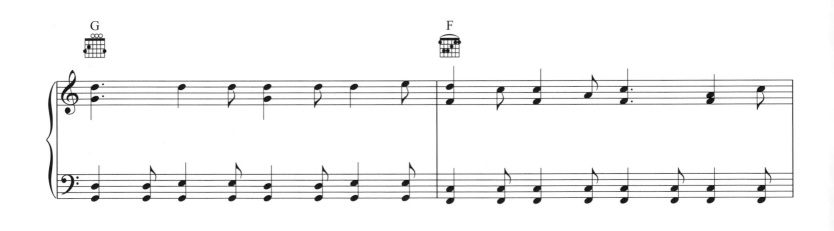

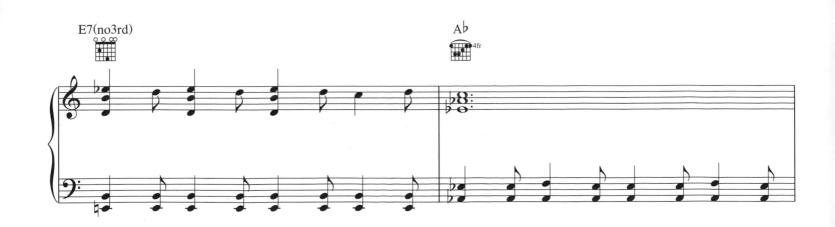

IT'S TOO LATE

Words and Music by CAROLE KING
and TONI STERN

Moderately slow

Stayed in bed all morn-in' just to pass the time. ___
used to be so eas-y, liv-in' here with you. ___

There's some-thin' wrong here, there can be no de-ny-in'. One of us ___ is chang-in', or
You were light and breez-y, an' I knew ___ just what to do. Now you look so un-hap-py, and I ___

may-be we've just ___ stopped try-in'. ___
___ feel ___ like a fool. ___

And it's too ___

JESSIE'S GIRL

Words and Music by
RICK SPRINGFIELD

Jes - sie is a friend; yeah, I know __
long with the cha - rade; there does-n't

__ he's been a good friend of mine. __ But late - ly some-thing's changed; __ it ain't hard __
seem to be a rea - son to change. __ You know, I feel __ so dirt - y when they start __

__ to de - fine: __ Jes - sie's got him - self a girl __ and I wan -
__ talk - in' cute; __ I wan - na tell her that I love __ her, but the

JUMP

Words and Music by DAVID LEE ROTH, EDWARD VAN HALEN,
ALEX VAN HALEN and MICHAEL ANTHONY

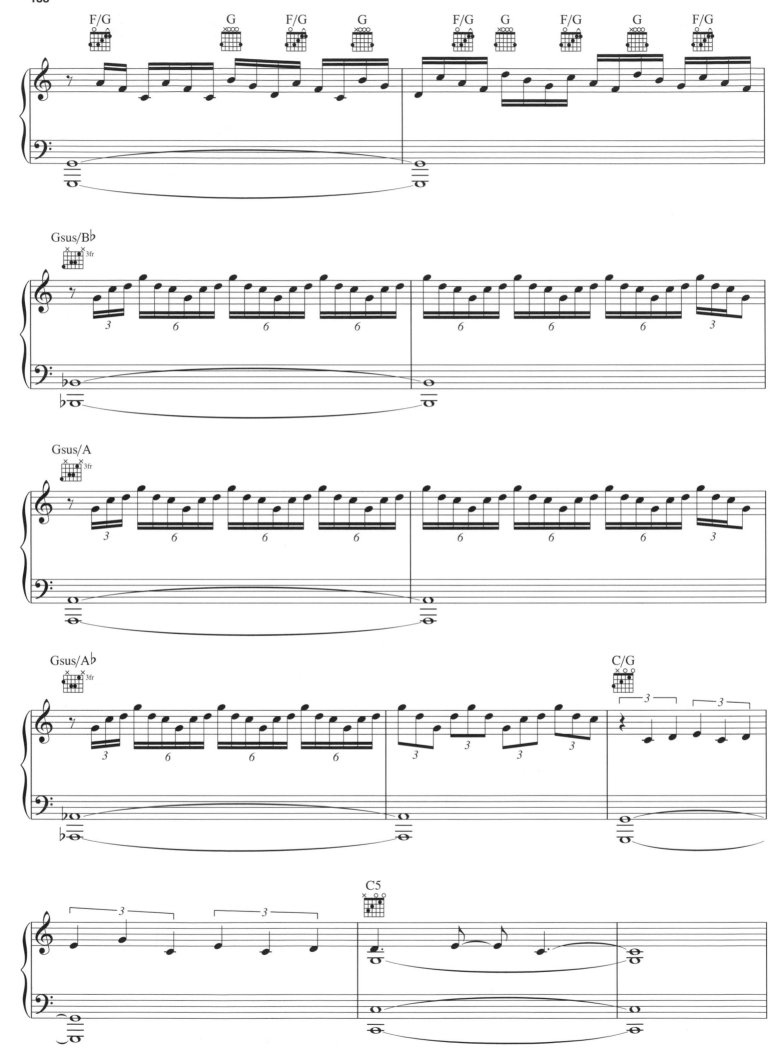

LADY

Words and Music by
LIONEL RICHIE

Moderately slow, with feeling

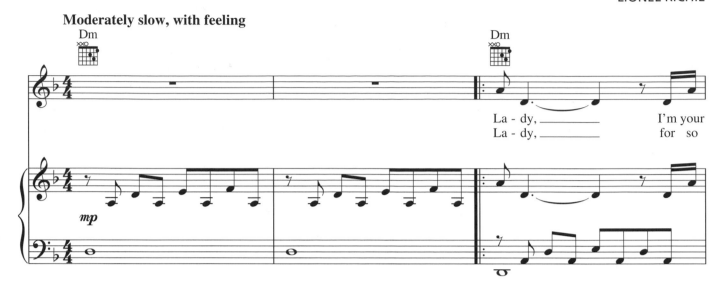

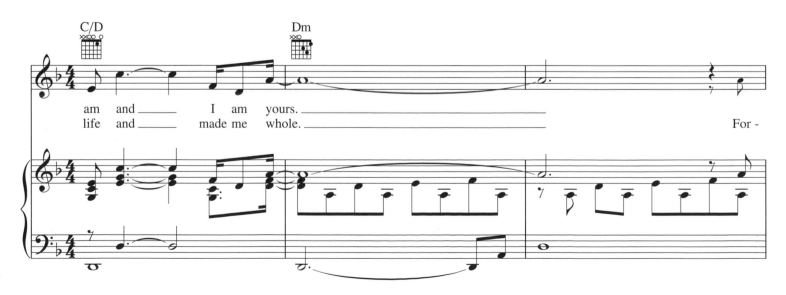

LIKE A VIRGIN

Words and Music by BILLY STEINBERG
and TOM KELLY

LIVIN' LA VIDA LOCA

Words and Music by ROBI ROSA
and DESMOND CHILD

She's in-to su-per-sti - tions, black cats and voo-doo dolls. __ I feel a prem-o-ni - tion. That girl's gon-na make me fall. __

OH, PRETTY WOMAN

Words and Music by ROY ORBISON
and BILL DEES

LIVIN' ON A PRAYER

Words and Music by JON BON JOVI,
RICHIE SAMBORA and DESMOND CHILD

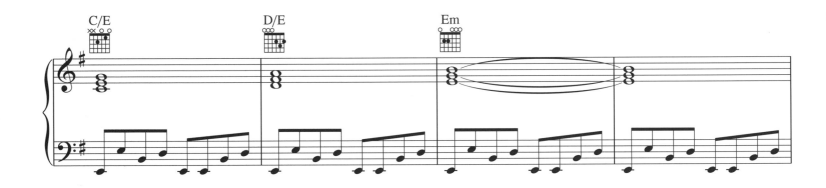

(Spoken:) Once upon a time, not so long ago...

Tom - my used to work on the docks, _____ un - ion's been on strike. He's
Tom - my's got his six - string in hock, _____ now he's hold - ing in what he

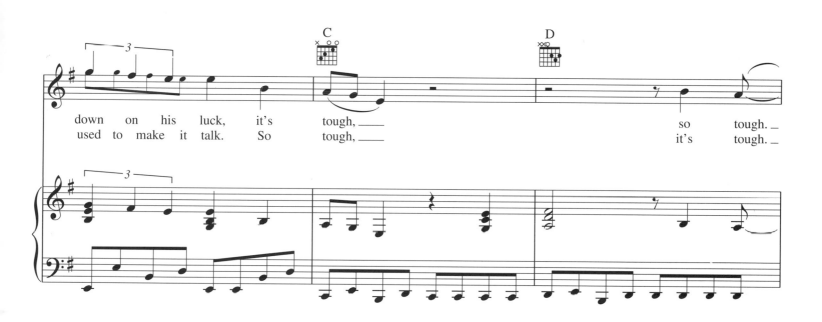

down on his luck, it's tough, _____ so tough. _
used to make it talk. So tough, _____ it's tough. _

Gi - na works the di - ner all day; _
Gi - na dreams of run - ning a - way; _

LOVE BITES

Words and Music by JOE ELLIOTT, PHIL COLLEN,
RICHARD SAVAGE, RICHARD ALLEN,
STEVE CLARK and ROBERT LANGE

2nd time Guitar solo

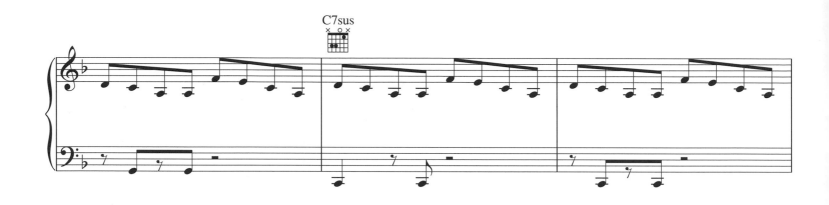

D.S. al Coda

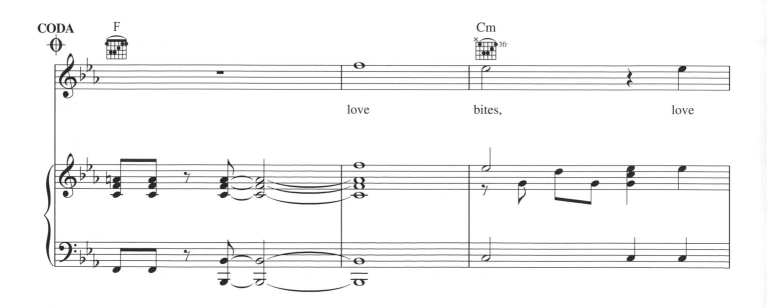

love   bites,   love

bleeds, it's bring-ing me to ___ my knees, ___ love

lives, love dies, it's no ___ sur-prise, ___ love

begs, love pleads. It's what I need. ___

Optional Ending

Repeat and Fade

LOVE WILL KEEP US TOGETHER

Words and Music by NEIL SEDAKA
and HOWARD GREENFIELD

Love,
You,
will

love will keep us to-geth-
you be-long to me —
be there to share for-ev-

- er;
now;
- er;

think of me, babe, when-ev - er
ain't gon-na set you free ___ now.
love will keep us to-geth - er.

some sweet - talk - in' guy _____ comes a - long, _____
When those guys start hang - in' a - round, _____
Said it be - fore and I'll say _____ it a - gain, _____ while

sing - in' his song. _____ Don't mess a - round; you
talk - in' me down, _____ hear with your heart and you
oth - ers pre - tend, _____ I need you now and

got - ta be strong. _____ } Just stop, 'cause I
won't hear a sound. _____ }
I'll need you then. _____ }

real - ly love ___ ya; stop, I'll be think - in' of ___ ya.

Look in my heart and let love keep us to - geth - er. ___

geth - er, ___

what - ev - er.

ONE SWEET DAY

Words and Music by MARIAH CAREY, WALTER AFANASIEFF,
SHAWN STOCKMAN, MICHAEL McCARY,
NATHAN MORRIS and WANYA MORRIS

SAY SAY SAY

Words and Music by PAUL McCARTNEY
and MICHAEL JACKSON

Say, say, _ say _____ what you want but don't play _____ games
go, go, _ go _____ where you want but don't leave _____ me
You, you, _ you _____ can nev-er say that I'm not _ the one

with my af-fec - tion. Take, take, _ take _____ what you need but
here for-ev - er. You, you, _ you _____ stay a - way, so
who real-ly loves_ you. I pray, pray, _ pray _____ ev-'ry day that

don't leave _____ me _____ with no di - rec - tion.
long, girl, _____ I _____ see you nev - er. What
you'll see _____ things, _____ girl, like I _____ do. What

All a - lone ___ I sit home by the phone ___ wait - ing
can I do, ___ girl, to get through to you? ___ 'Cause I
can I do, ___ girl, to get through to you? ___ 'Cause I

for _ you, ba - by. Through the years _ how can you
love _ you, ba - by. Stand - ing here _ bap-tised in
love _ you, ba - by. Stand - ing here _ bap-tised in

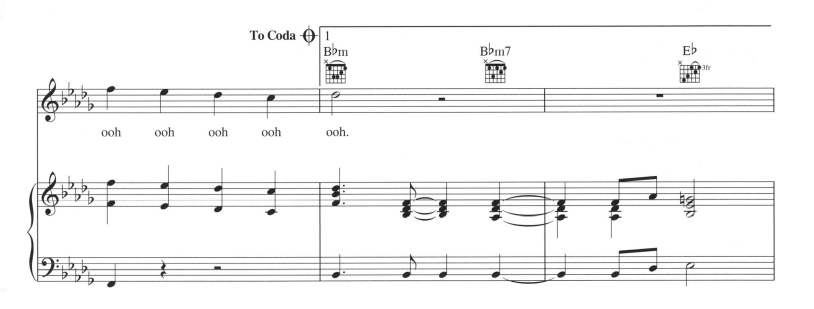

SAVE THE BEST FOR LAST

Words and Music by PHIL GALDSTON,
JON LIND and WENDY WALDMAN

Just when I thought _____ our chance _ had passed, _

_____ you go and save _____ the best _____ for last. _

All of the nights _____ _____

SAVING ALL MY LOVE FOR YOU

Words by GERRY GOFFIN
Music by MICHAEL MASSER

SAY YOU, SAY ME

Words and Music by
LIONEL RICHIE

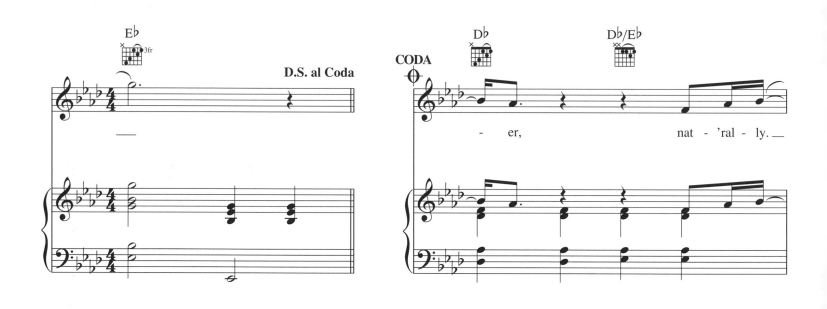

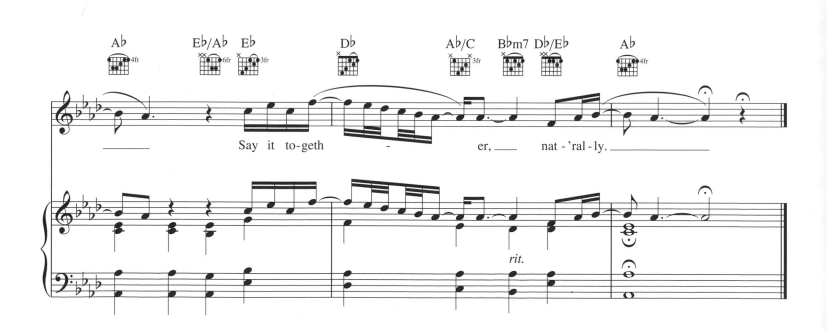

SMOOTH

Words by ROB THOMAS
Music by ROB THOMAS and ITAAL SHUR

(Just Like)
STARTING OVER

Words and Music by
JOHN LENNON

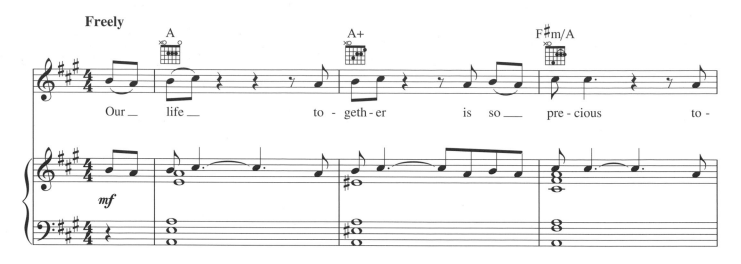

Freely

Our __ life __ to - geth - er is so __ pre - cious to -

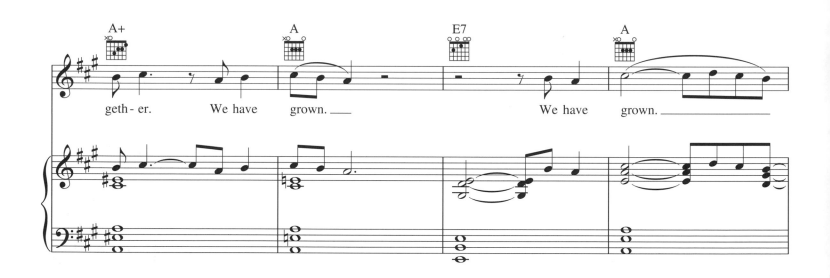

geth - er. We have grown. __ We have grown. _____

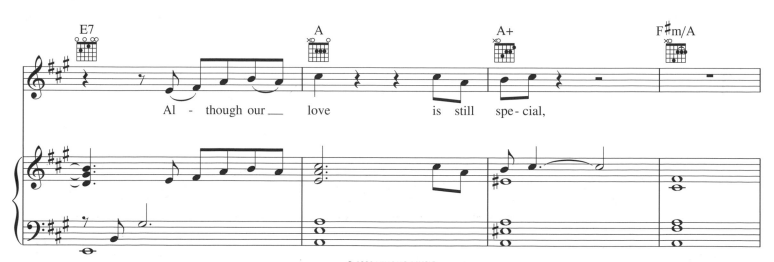

Al - though our __ love is still spe - cial,

TONIGHT'S THE NIGHT
(Gonna Be Alright)

Words and Music by
ROD STEWART

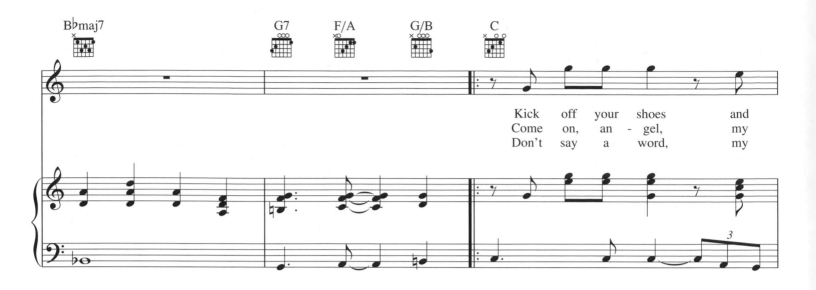

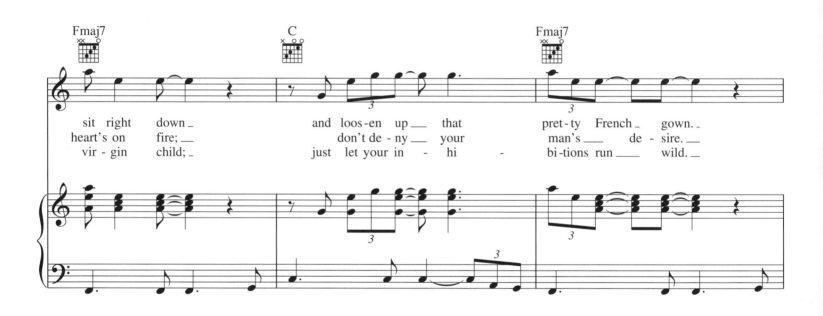

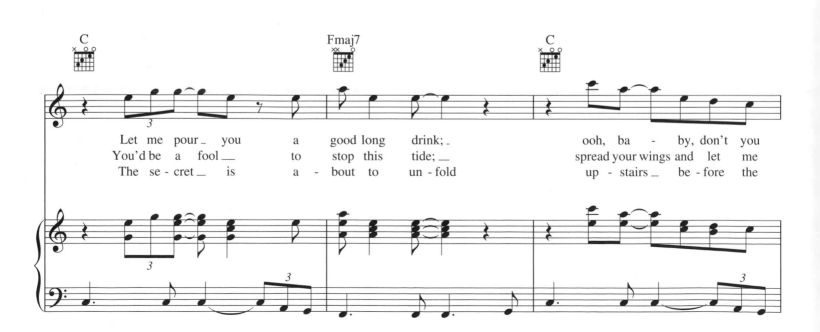

TOP OF THE WORLD

Words and Music by JOHN BETTIS
and RICHARD CARPENTER

Such a feel - in's com - in' o - ver me. _____
Some - thing in ___ the wind has learned _ my name. _____

THE WAY WE WERE

Words by ALAN and MARILYN BERGMAN
Music by MARVIN HAMLISCH

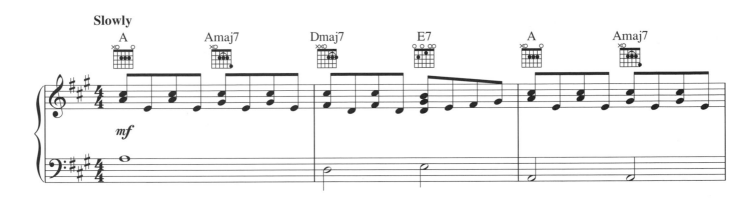

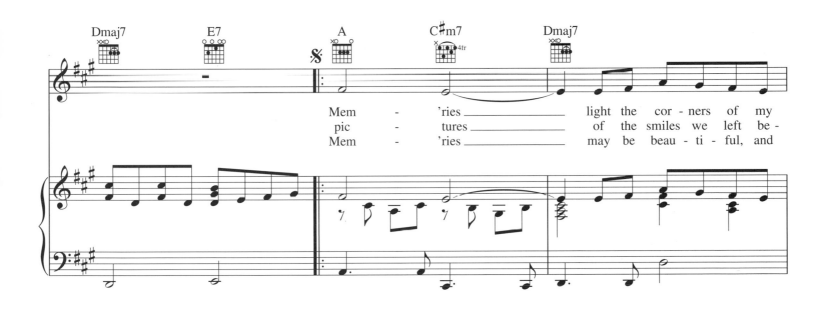

Mem - 'ries _____ light the cor - ners of my
pic - tures _____ of the smiles we left be -
Mem - 'ries _____ may be beau - ti - ful, and

mind.
hind,   smiles we gave to one an - oth - er
yet,   what's too pain - ful to re - mem - ber

Mist - y wa - ter - col - or mem - 'ries _____
er _____
ber _____

UP WHERE WE BELONG

from the Paramount Picture AN OFFICER AND A GENTLEMAN

Words by WILL JENNINGS
Music by BUFFY SAINTE-MARIE and JACK NITZSCHE

WHEN DOVES CRY

Composed by PRINCE

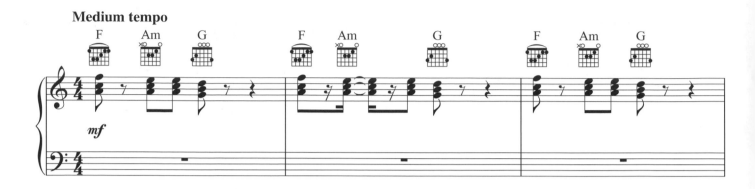

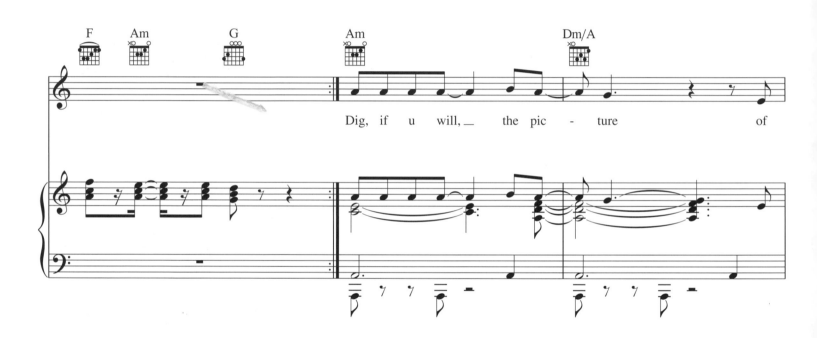

THE POP/ROCK ERA

Hal Leonard is proud to present these fantastic folios that gather the best popular songs from the '50s to today! All books arranged for piano, voice, and guitar.

THE POP/ROCK ERA: THE '50s

54 highlights from the first official decade of the pop/rock revolution, including: All Shook Up • At the Hop • Don't Be Cruel (To a Heart That's True) • Donna • Get a Job • Great Balls of Fire • Hound Dog • It's So Easy • Kansas City • (You've Got) Personality • That'll Be the Day • Why Do Fools Fall in Love • and more.
00310788................................$14.95

THE POP/ROCK ERA: THE '60s

52 songs that helped shape the pop/rock era, including: Baby Love • Can't Take My Eyes off of You • Crying • Fun, Fun, Fun • Hey Jude • I Heard It Through the Grapevine • I Think We're Alone Now • Louie, Louie • Mony, Mony • Respect • Stand by Me • Stop! In the Name of Love • Wooly Bully • and more.
00310789................................$14.95

THE POP/ROCK ERA: THE '70s

44 of the top songs from the '70s, including: ABC • Baby, I Love Your Way • Bohemian Rhapsody • Don't Cry Out Loud • Fire and Rain • I Love the Night Life • Imagine • Joy to the World • Just My Imagination (Running Away with Me) • The Logical Song • Oye Como Va • Piano Man • Three Times a Lady • We've Only Just Begun • You Are So Beautiful • and more.
00310790................................$14.95

THE POP/ROCK ERA: THE '80s

38 top pop hits from the '80s, including: Back in the High Life Again • Centerfold • Every Breath You Take • Eye in the Sky • Higher Love •Summer of '69 • Sweet Dreams (Are Made of This) • Thriller • Time After Time • and more.
00310791................................$14.95

THE POP/ROCK ERA: THE '90s

35 hits that shaped pop music in the 1990s, including: All I Wanna Do • Angel • Come to My Window • (Everything I Do) I Do It for You • Fields of Gold • From a Distance • Hard to Handle • Hero • I Will Remember You • Mambo No. 5 (A Little Bit Of...) • My Heart Will Go On (Love Theme from 'Titanic') • Ray of Light • Tears in Heaven • When She Cries and more.
00310792................................$14.95

Prices, contents and availability subject to change without notice.

FOR MORE INFORMATION, SEE YOUR LOCAL MUSIC DEALER, OR WRITE TO:

HAL•LEONARD®
CORPORATION
7777 W. BLUEMOUND RD. P.O. BOX 13819 MILWAUKEE, WI 53213

www.halleonard.com